LEARN THE ALPHABET

with the

MUNCH BUNCH

Library of Congress in Publication Data

Reed, Giles.
  Learn the alphabet with the Munch Bunch.

  Summary: The Munch Bunch engage in various
activities using objects with names beginning with
each letter of the alphabet.
  1. English language—Alphabet—Juvenile litera-
ture. [1. Alphabet] I. Mitson, Angela, ill.
II. Title.
PE1155.R43 1981   [E]   81-12074
ISBN 0-86625-075-1   AACR2

Rourke Publications, Inc.
Windermere, FL   32786

Aa

Pedro Orange is asleep. **Can you see…**
apple airplane arrow avocado axe
artist ant anchor apron acorn

Bb

On the beach. Can you see...
balloon book blackberry bucket
boat basket box

Cc **Olly Onion is** crying. **Can you see...**
clock carrot canoe cup
case celery cushion comb cake

Dd

Scruff is dirty, as usual. Can you see...
drum drawer dress drink door
daffodil doll dish dice

Ee

Sally is eating **a biscuit. Can you see...**
ears engine easel elephant eyes
envelope earring egg elbow eclair

Ff

Pippa is frying **dinner. Can you see…**
fork fish fire fence fireworks
frog fan flower flag feather

Gg

Flowers are growing. **Can you see...**
glass gingerbread guitar glove garden
gate greenhouse gun gooseberry gift

Hh

Billy Blackberry is happy. **Can you see...**
ham hedgehog horn hammer
handkerchief hat hill handbag horse

Zack Zucchini is juggling. **Can you see…**
igloo jeep icicle jelly
jewels invitation jar ice cream jug

Kk

Spud is kissing Lizzie. Can you see...

king knife knight kilt kite
kettle key knitting knee kitten

 **Lucy is** licking **her** lollypop. **Can you see...**
log lantern ladder letter
leek lane leg leaf lemon

Mm

A merry **time of year. Can you see...**
mouse motor cycle milk mushroom match
mop mistletoe mince pie moon money box

Having fun outside. **Can you see...**
needle nut newspaper nose nest
onion overall oar oil can orange

Pp

Bursting purple **balloons. Can you see...**
paint brush plate pin pear picture
palette pencil plant parsnip patch

Pete is lying quietly **in bed. Can you see...**
quilt queue queen quarter quill
rolling pin rake rainbow rain

Peanut is sailing **his boat. Can you see...**
seesaw sandwich spider spoon stone
swing saucer sausage sun strawberry

Tt

Time for a cup of tea. Can you see...
tomato tooth-paste teapot tree torch
toothbrush table tent tortoise towel

A visit to a tennis match. Can you see...
umbrella urn umpire ukelele uniform
vest vase violet van violin

Lizzie is washing **Scruff. Can you see...**

Ww

watering can worm water wasp wood
wheel watch windmill whistle window

Slippy Banana is yawning. **Can you see…**
x-ray xylophone yak yoyo yacht
yolk yogurt zebra zip zither

Ch Chunky is chopping wood. Can you see...
cheese chair chisel check chopper
church chest chart chopstick chip

Sh Peanut is shootin
shield shadow
shed shell shawl

ater. Can you see...

hoe shovel shirt
hark ship

Th Supercool is thirsty. Can you see...

thatch three thicket thrush thirteen
thumb thread throat thimble

TOM'S TEAM 13
SPUD'S TEAM 3

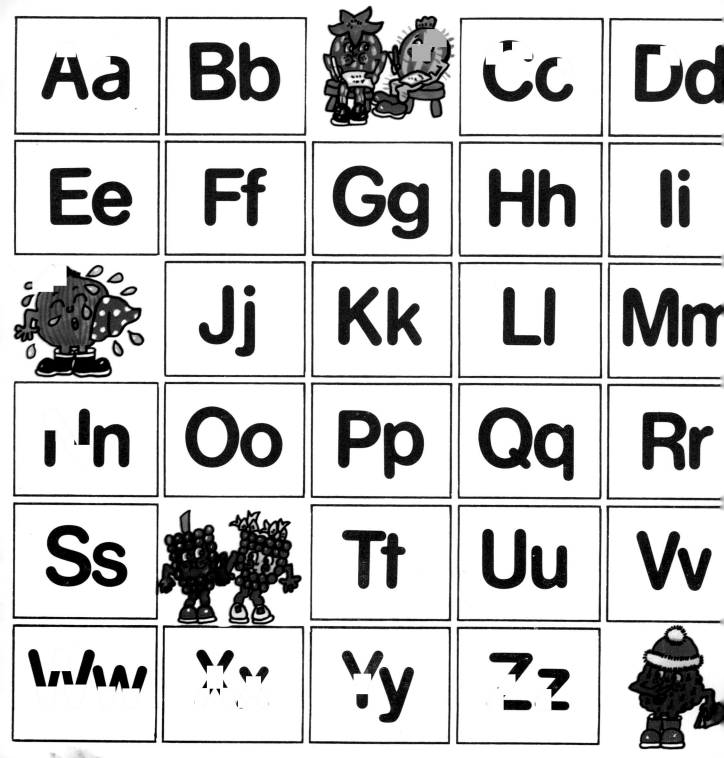